The Sin_g---_g ------ --

Poems By
Frank Stanford

Lost Roads Number 18
1979, 2008 (2nd Printing)

Some of these poems appeared in the following
publications, to whom acknowledgement is here
made:
THE CHICAGO REVIEW, THE FAR POINT
(Canada), KAYAK, THE LITTLE REVIEW, THE
MASSACHUSETTS REVIEW, THE MILL
MOUNTAIN REVIEW, THE NATION, THE
NEW AMERICAN REVIEW, OPEN PLACES,
THE WEST COAST REVIEW (Canada).

Stanford, Frank
        The Singing Knives

        (Lost Roads; no. 18)

PS3569.T3316S5   811'.5'4   78-17914
ISBN-10: 0-918786-19-3
ISBN-13: 978-0-918786-55-5

Published by Lost Roads Publishing Company
First Edition published by Mill Mountain Press
(Irv Broughton, publisher) 1972
Printed in Canada

Cover Photo by Susan Bank
Interior Design by Vera Donovan
Cover Design by Kat Hodges

CONTENTS

The Singing Knives

THE BLOOD BROTHERS

There was Born In The Camp With Six Toes
He popped the cottonmouth's head off

There was Baby Gauge
He tied the line to his wrist
He tied it to the alligator gar
He rode the fish

There was Ray Baby
He stole the white man's gold tooth
He knocked it out with a two-by-four
He rode the moon-blind horse

There was Charlie B. Lemon
He had four wives and a pair
Of long-toed shoes

There was Mose Jackson
He threw snake eyes in his sleep

There was BoBo Washington
A rat crawled in the bed
And sucked the blood
Out of his baby's head

There was Jimmy
He had the knife like night
He was white

I had the hands like dragonflies
I killed one white man

He was a midget
I did it with a frog gig
It was the summer of the Chinese daughter
I danced on the levee

1964

THE SINGING KNIVES

The dogs woke me up
I looked out the window

Jimmy ran down the road
With the knife in his mouth
He was naked
And the moon
Was a dead man floating down the river

He jumped on the Gypsy's pony
He rode through camp
I could see the dust

There was the saddlebag full of knives
He was crazy

When Jimmy cut a throat
The eyes rolled back in the head
Like they was baptized
I tell you
When he cut a throat
It was like Abednego's guitar
And the blood
Flew out like a quail

He had the red hand
He poked the eyes out

I dreamed I stepped over a log
And there was fire in my foot
I dreamed I saw a turkey and two wildcats
Jumped on me at the same time
I dreamed Jimmy was pouring ice water

Over my head at noon
I dreamed I heard somebody
Singing in the outhouse
I dreamed the mad dog bit the Gypsy
And they tied him to a tree
I dreamed I was buried in the Indian mound
And Moon Lake rose up
I dreamed my father was wading the river of death
With his heart in his hand
I dreamed Jimmy rowed out the front door
With a hawk on his shoulder
And I was in the bow kneeling down
I dreamed the blacksnake rode the guitar
Down the river
I dreamed the clouds went by
The moon like dead fish
I dreamed I was dragging
A cotton sack with a dead man in it
I dreamed the fish bandits stole the hogs
Off my lines
And one of them was a hunchback
I dreamed the night was a horse
With its eyes shut
I dreamed I had to fight the good man with the bad arm
And he had the dynamite
I dreamed I trailed a buck from Panther Brake to
Panther Burn
I dreamed the Chickasaw slit his throat in the papaw
I dreamed that rising sun was smoking blood
You could pick up and throw
I dreamed the Chinamen's peg leg
I dreamed I was fishing in heaven with Sho Nuff
and Jesus cleaned the fish

I dreamed a man flies wouldn't bite
I dreamed I was riding through Leland in a dragline
bucket
And the cotton making everyday
I dreamed we got the bootlegger's truck out of the mud
I dreamed the levee broke
I dreamed the Gypsy was laughing under the water
And the minnows were swimming through his eyes
I dreamed I reached down in Moon Lake
And untied his arms and one hand
Floated up the way it did
When he threw those knives
I dreamed the pony that fights in the water
And the boat that towed the dead man
I dreamed I felt the knife singing in Abednego's back
I dreamed I pulled the ring out of his ear
And Jimmy put it on his finger
And swam through the water
I dreamed he was looking for Abednego's boot
And when he came up
He had the jackknife between his teeth
I dreamed he was so beautiful
He had to die someday
I dreamed a knife like a song you can't whistle

"Let's go, I got to throw tonight" he says

He had the bandanna around his neck
And the pilot's cap on
He played the harp in the moonlight

I led the horse out back
I tied him to the Chinaberry tree

11

"What you want" I says
But I knew he wanted me
Standing at the back of that outhouse
"Shut up" he says "don't move"

The dirt dobbers flew around my head

He threw Boo Kay Jack at me
He threw Django at me

The mosquitoes drew blood
I looked on the ground
I saw the shadows coming like gars
Swimming under me at night
I saw the red moon too
I wished I was running a trot line
I wished I was in a fight
I wished I was fanning myself in church
But there was a heart on the fan
With a switchblade through it

And the knives came by

The bone handled one
The hawk handled one
The one with a blade like a skiff
Out of his boot
Behind his back
Mexican style
The way Abednego showed him

Singing in the outhouse
Like a horse breaking wind

He took the knife and ran it
Across his arm
Then he ran it across mine

Blood come out like hot soda

He tied our arms together
With the blue bandana
And we laid down in the cotton
I wished I was riding a mule somewhere
Blowing a jug
With a string full of crappie
And the cotton making everyday

LIVING

I had my quiet time early in the morning
Eating Almond Joys with Mother.
We'd sit on the back porch and talk to God.
We really had a good time.

Later on,
I'd sort baseball cards
Or look for bottles.
In the afternoon I'd shoot blackbirds.

Jimmy would go by the house for ice water
And make the truck backfire.
Oh, I really liked that.
That was the reason he did it.

In the evening the cottontails ran across the groves.
I shot one and put him in the backseat.
He went to the bathroom.
Jimmy said I knocked the shit out of him.

At night we would listen to the ballgame.
Then to the Hoss Man.
Jimmy liked "Take Out Some Insurance On Me Baby"
        by Jimmy Reed.

THE PUMP

There was always a lizard
Or a frog around the pump,
Waiting for a little extra water
Or a butterfly to light.

Jimmy said the pump gave him the worms.
I got the worms under the slick boards.
The pump would bite you in the winter.
It got hold of Jimmy and wouldn't let go.

The blades of Johnson grass were tall
And sharp around the pump stand.
I had to hoe them all the time
Nobody filled the prime jar, though.

One time, I cut the tongue
Out of a Buster Brown shoe
And gave it to the pump.
It made a good sucker washer.

Sometimes, the pump seemed like Jesus.
I liked bathing buck naked
Under the pump,
Not in the goddamn washtub.

THE GOSPEL BIRD

I Superman

Dressed in a superman suit
On the front porch of Chitum's store
I told all the Negroes "I can fly"
And jumped off the high end.

A German crop duster crashed.
A chicken ran out of the hole
And shit on a rusty three-penny nail,
Then ducked under the stoop.

Blood and chickenshit
Dripping out of the hole
Into the good hand,
Jimmy says, "What you saving it for?"

He went to the fire
And nobody was studying me
But toad frogs and a dog.
"Whoa somebody! I done cut my hand off."

Nobody came but the Rollie Pollie man,
Skipping cuck-holes and swinging coal oil
In a copper-wired Coca-cola bottle.
He says, "I'll tend to you boy, I'll tend to you."

II Fire

Chitum's cripple nigger carpenter
Ate porch bugs and did magic.
He had a police dog that brought him
Dead chickens in the night.

"Put hog lard on an oak tree,
Steal me whiskey and coal oil,
And this dog will bring your chicken back."
I wanted that bird.

"Lock Jaw and penicillin all the same,
Kill the chicken to kill the pain."
I got the nigger a fifth of gin
And he sent his dog after the bird.

The Rollie Pollie man told me how it was:
"The blood spurt out when that son-of-a-bitch
Chitum blew my crooked-necked
Chicken-killing dog in half.

"Black gnats was dying in the blood,
Some already drowned, I took coat wire
And drug him deep into the Diamond Woods."
My hand and Chitum's store burned that night.

III Fly Away, Fly Away

My father talked like he was singing
When he bought the burnt-out land and store,
But all I cared about was
The one thousand chickens in the deal.

He said to kill all the birds
And sell the meat to the levee camps
Up and down the river.
The Rollie Pollie man was on the run.

Jimmy was wringing their necks
And making a clean kill,
But I was knocking
Their heads off with a tomato stick

Everytime I connected
I'd go check the bird out.
They'd bat their wings and squirt blood,
Winking at me.

I was busting green heads off ducks, too.
Jimmy had to hold me back.
"What's wrong with you, Superman?"
"Fly away, fly away, Gospel Bird," I cried.

ALBINO

"I'm afraid of you, MacCulduff,"
I told my father's foreman.
He rubbed pomade on his face
And put the headdress of an Arab on.
"Get in the boat," he said and smiled.

The albino was a strange man
Who spoke like an Indian
And looked like a real angel
Until he opened his mouth.
"You only have two teeth," I said.

MacCulduff handed me his pole
And told me to put it together.
The only light we had was lightning.
"Don't stick a hook in your finger."
He yawned like a hawk spreading its beak.

"In an hour there will be a sun."
He took a tiger moth from the thole pin
And threw it in the river.
"I don't know about other things,
But fishing will be good today."
The low water and the fog in the swamps
Made the cypress knees look like tombstones.
The old lines of other fishermen
Were snagged around them.
"What have the old men made you do?"
"Rip off my shirt and dip it in deer blood,
Chew the red wattle of a Tom gobbler,
And swallow a fish eye, MacCulduff."
"I was made to cut the throat of a fawn
And wear its blood for a week," he said.

19

MacCulduff worked the paddle like a spoon
Stirring some brew. He feathered it so well,
Turkeys above us shit in the boat.
"Tell me boy, what strange things have you seen?"
"I saw three things yesterday, MacCulduff:
A blind rabbit, a cow peeing on its calf,
And a snake on a power line."
"I have seen all that, " the albino said.
Switchwillows dropped a heavy dew
Down my neck and whipped back into his face.
Sometimes, they got so thick, I couldn't see
The boat, MacCulduff, or the water.
"You hear a boat back there? You hear?"
He shook his head and said, "Mosquitoes."
"Shoot man, it's getting dark out here, not light.
When are we going to get to the hole?"
With a willow resting on his neck,
MacCulduff lifted the scull from the swamp
And struck three matches for his limpsy roll,
Then looked at the dark east and rubbed his joints.

       "Listen out there," he said.
Buono! Buono! The Italians yelled *Buono!*
As they hauled in their nets from the river.
I listened to the Dago fishermen
Sing to the fish in the lightning
And saw the place close up for the first time.
The hole was like a lake in a forest,
With fog way up in the cypress tops,
And the fish after gadflies sounded
Like someone shooting a Twenty-Two.
"This morning it smells like a lady," he said.
And hung from thunder, a moccasin

With four fangs fell into the boat.
MacCulduff grinned at the snake,
Then broke its neck with the scull
When it crawled towards the gunnel.
Tornadoes hit the country that afternoon;
And while MacCulduff was scaling a fish,
The point of a knife, twenty years old,
Began working its way out of his knee.

ELEGY FOR MY FATHER
1883 - 1963

When Alfalfa was afraid,
Spanky and Buckwheat
Put a gar in his sock
And said it was his leg.
Everyone thought he was sick;
He sang in the bed all night long.

The devil was beating his wife
In the Bear Creek Woods
And I was alone
In the roots of a cypress tree.

I had one finger in my ear
and one in my toes looking for jam,
Waiting for the Negroe
To set off the dynamite.

There were coons in the mussels
And sticks of powder
Under every stump.
Toadspit was washing off the weeds.

A fish head was nailed to each tree.
And the gar bladders going down
Sounded like a thousand slow leaks.
A kingfisher dived for the river;
Fish bladders and dynamite began to blow up.

I saw half a bullfrog
Fly under the rainbow
And land on the bank.

It hopped for the rest of itself.
It hopped for the rest of its life.

The devil is beating his wife
In the Bear Creek Woods;
Alfalfa sings in the bed
With his gar leg on;
My father's socks sit in the drawer
Like old bullfrogs.

TAPSTICKS

In hornbeam woods only jug men would see
I would climb sixty feet in the sycamores
And skin the grey branches like rabbits
Then throw them down to the Negroes below
White and slick as a catfish belly
The limbs were light and untrue
Unless we drove a nail through a washer
At the end nails were the hard part
The woods were all over

        Baby Gauge   Jimmy
Born in The Camp With Six Toes   and I
Walked the bank for run-up barges
The cypress barges put together   way back
With spikes and pitch   before we were born
Trapped when the cut-off changed the river's course
When we found one   the sink mud around it
We took turns letting each other down
Through the rotting bow with the tapsticks
Saying to each other "Quick! Let me down quick!"
Sometimes seeing a moccasin move
In the bilge   by the light
That broke   through the holes in the deck
Sucking blue gook to our navels and necks
We smelled bellies in the dead river's mud
And pulled ourselves up to the sun to dry
Back on the bank snake doctors tending to us
We beat the sticks in the old boat's pitch
And watched the bulrush wave   on the other side
So once out of trees and river wind
The jugs pulling against the current
And the earth cracking
On our backs for protection

We'd leave cudwood and cottonwood   behind
With the new tapsticks
Held up high and balanced well
To look for rabbits on the levee
Butterflies lighting on our butts and on
The sticks too   hands over our mouths   squealing
Listening for cottontails stop and start
Within the same circle of flight
Crossing the barr pit   cane brake   and tangles
Of honeysuckle   their white tails weaving
Through the joe-pye and jimson weed
We'd break into deer jumps   tapsticks high
Leaving our blood and wind in the buckthorns
"Hello! Brother Rabbit!" someone would yell
And we all let loose with the long white sticks
Blood   new mud   and broken breath we
Ran to the spot to see what we had

They stood behind me as I bent over
In their shadows smelling its breath like oatmeal
The tapsticks' shadows rising   I turned
Towards the sun and saw Jimmy's gold tooth
And the blood on the washer shine
Smiling he pointed towards the cottontail
Pumping the buckshot dirt with its lucky foot
Working around like Harpo Marx

THE BASS

He jumps up high
against the night,
rattling his gills
and the hooks
in his back.
The Indian says
he is like a goose
passing in front
of the moon.

THE NOCTURNAL SHIPS OF THE PAST

There was always a great darkness

moving out
like a forest of arrows

So many ships in the past

their bows bearing women
as stalks bear eyes

The burning ships
that drove their bowsprits
between the thighs of dreams

With my ear to the ground
I hear the black prows coming

plowing the night
into water

and the wind comes up
and I smell the sour wood

leaving a wake I want to be
left alone with

Night after night

like a sleeping knife that runs deep
through the belly
the tomb ships come

1971

THE MINNOW

If I press
on its head,
the eyes
will come out
like stars.
The ripples
it makes
can move
the moon.

THE PICTURE SHOW NEXT DOOR TO THE STAMP STORE IN DOWNTOWN MEMPHIS

The movie has not begun.
Girls from a private school
are forming their lines.
They have long socks on,
tweed skirts, blue weskits,
berets. The colors
of God and their school
are sewn in their scarfs.

My money and my hand
are in a machine.
The cup does not come down,
but the ice and cola do.
I make a cup with my hands.

They stand there, moving
in one direction
like does in clover.
The nun tells them to form.

Why are they afraid of me?

I am holding my hands together
like a gloveless hunter
drinking water in the morning
or calling up owls in the forest;
I am holding my hands together
like a hunter in winter
with his hands in the water
washing away my blood.

Outside, a man with a lunch box
walks past the marquee.
His new stamps
fly out of his hands;
orange triangles from San Salvador
fly into the traffic.
I am holding my hands
like the nun.

Then fly over Front Street.
He is looking up;
other people are looking up.
The stamps tremble
like the butterflies
from the Yazoo Basin
stuck to the radiator
of my father's car.

The girls are in the seventh grade.
The backs of their thighs
and their foreheads are damp.

What are they learning?
Ballet? French?

The nun is on her toes.

Their booties dance
in the leotards,
rounding out like the moon.
They are making a debut.

The girls are following the nun
into the dark.

The movie is beginning.
The lid on the machine
comes down like a guillotine.

POEM

When the rain hits the snake in the head,
he closes his eyes and wishes he were
asleep in a tire on the side of the road,
so young boys could roll him over, forever.

TRANSCENDENCE OF JANUS

I am not asleep, but I see
a limb, the fingers of death, the ghost
of an anonymous painter
leaving the prints of death
on the wall; the bright feathers
of soft birds blowing
away in the forest;
the bones of fish and
the white backs of strange women;
your breathing
like the slow thunder
on the other side of some river
as you sleep beside me; old
dancing teachers weeping in their offices;
toads with bellies as quiet
as girls asleep in mansions, dreaming
of saddles and pulling the sheets
between their legs; fireflies
going to sleep on moonseed flowers
around a plantation gazebo at dawn;
a girl sweating in bed; hawks drifting
through the moon; a woman's hair,
the flavor of death, floating
in the fog like a flag
on a ship full of ghosts,
the ghosts of soldiers
searching for the graves of their mothers; june bugs
listening to Leoncavallo;
christ weeping on Coney Island,
inevitable, like a fissure
in a faggot's ass; a widower

with no sons, a lonesome janitor,
a worm in the sun, the dusty sockets
of poets, who have lost their eyes, their

STRAPPADO

I was thinking about back then
before I thought I
heard chords on a flute
when there was no young bird
beating its wings inside my belly
no light in my eyes
This was long ago
before the wise shadows
of the fantoccini
commanded the land
when the moon
was the blind eye of a fish
in the back of a cave

IF I SHOULD WAKE

Sleeping on a willow raft
in a quiet inlet –
the feathergrass
carries the shapes
of wolves, as though there were
a stillness in the night,
wet and heavy,
like the tongue of a buck
or a root. It glows
in the incomplete
skeletons of crayfish,
and in their claws
detached in battle, left
behind like footprints.
It is also present
in the nocturnal eyes
of snails.

If I should wake,
I would see the blue bones
of crayfish rise up
and return
to their osseous claws,
walk into the shadows
of themselves,
reared on the shore,
turned red to brush
the clean whiskers
of the beast, forever.

There are wagons
passing in the night,

crushing the wands of snails.
A Choctaw dreaming in his tent.

WISHING MY WIFE HAD ONE LEG

Caryatid with eyes of nails
　　　always being driven
with thighs of a canoe
　　　and of horses fighting
with the back of nine maidens drowning
Caryatid with the hair of a flag
　　　raised in battle
with the thoughts of a severed member
　　　and of orphans sleeping
with nipples of amethyst on lifted chalices
Carytid with the neck of a bow
　　　drawn towards the forest
with the sex of a ship coming about
　　　and of a wing in a bamboo cage
with the voice of a silent chisel
Caryatid with the heart of a feather

NARCISSUS TO ACHILLES

Yesterday, I passed over a bridge
and saw a boot underwater.
Such thought I had,
I cannot tell you.

BERGMAN THE BURNING SHIP

I swim
through the cold and open blood of bandits
one-armed with a ghost sword
and a boy with a wounded hand
his curls in my teeth
his neck in my mouth
we make for the burning deck
this child
part bear like myself
who calls me "Bee Wolfe"
I who have towed my tomb ship
out of the earth
to set us both afire
again
with my song
so the boy can
bite down on the rope
so I can say "Swim my son
tow me through the poison waters"
with my spirit
standing at the prow
see me asleep a bending fire
and I will unlock my hoard of dreams
and give them all to you
I will bestow them like rings
but keep an eye
out for those who would wield
their glory behind your back
and loot your heart O
I know the prows
that crossed mine
Hunting
the bloodsucker

who double-crossed me with that blade
I don't remember
there was the often-sung sword of the gods
that melted
down to the hilt
there was one called Ing
and when it failed
I knew I was meant to drain the blood cup
alone
but I used my own sword Naegling once more
my beloved blade
it betrayed me too
it broke into firewood
a kindling I'll always recall
by god the hug of my arm
was stronger than any weapon
it is not meant for men
to wield glory"
I sing of my wake a burning masthead
and a son like a swan
I with tributaries of night
on my lips and the silent
she-wolves of a river in my heart
I know
no man can forge sword to grip
my hand

PLANNING THE DISAPPEARANCE
OF THOSE WHO HAVE GONE

Soon I will make my appearance
But first I must take off my rings
And sword and lay them out all
Along the lupine banks of the forbidden river
In reckoning the days I have
Left on this earth I will use
No fingers

THE INTRUDER

after Jean Follain

In the evenings they listen to the same
tunes nobody could call happy
somebody turns up at the edge of town
the roses bloom
and an old dinner bell rings once more
under the thunder clouds
In front of the porch posts of the store
a man seated on a soda water case
turns around and spits and says
to everybody
in his new set of clothes
holding up his hands
as long as I live nobody
touches my dogs my friends

THE QUIVER

Come back dull and bloody all of you
let it hold the shame inside
itself like a helmet
bring a little soil each time
for a pillow
you aren't as many as you were

BECOMING THE UNICORN

Go away virgin
if I lay my head
in your lap too long
they will come and lay
a knife in mine

BELLADONNA

The night I met you
I had the black shirt on
I had the ice pick in my boot

I climbed the tree buck naked
I swung out on a limb

I swam all the way
Under the water
With the knife in my mouth

Like a song of hog blood
Footprints you cannot track

A song that comes apart
Like a rosary
In the back of a church

O bootblack the night I met you
I quit shining shoes

THE SNAKE DOCTORS *for Nicholas Fuhrmann*

I Pig

I was in the outhouse
I heard somebody at the pump
I looked out the chink hole
It was the two fisherman
They stole fish

One man gave the other one some money
He flipped a fifty-cent piece up
I lost it in the sun
I saw the snake doctors riding each other
The other man said "You lose"
He took something else out of his pocket
It shined
They had a tow sack
I thought they were cleaning fish
I looked up
I saw the snake doctors riding each other

I took my eye away
It was dark in the outhouse
I whistled

I heard the pump again
It sounded broken
I looked out the chink hole
It wasn't the pump
It was the pig

The guitar player cut them out
The midget helped him
"Pump me some water, midget" he said

The pig ran off
The guitar player washed off his hands
The midget washed off the nuts
He got a drink
My eye hurt

He laughed
He cleaned the blood off his knife   He wiped
      it on his leg
He started singing
The dog tried to get the nuts
But the midget kicked him

The guitar player picked them up
He put them in his pocket
The dog went over to the pig
He licked him

I pulled my pants up
I went outside

I got the pig
I walked over to the pump
I said "Don't you ever lay a hand
      on this pig again"
The guitar player laughed

He asked me if I wanted the nuts back
He took them out of his pocket
He spit on them
He shook them like dice
He threw them on the ground
He said "Hah"

The midget stomped on them
I had the pig under my arm
He was bleeding on my foot   I said
"Midget, I got friends on that river"

II The Acolyte

The men rode by

I passed them on the road
They smelled like dead fish

The one in front had a guitar on his back
The other one had a chain saw

I was riding the hog
He weighed three-hundred pounds
I called him Holy Ghost

The midget flashed a knife
He thumbed the blade
He smiled at me
He called me "Pig rider"

I rode over to Baby Gauge's
I was on my way to church
I had to get the red cassock
I tied the hog to the front porch
Baby Gauge was swinging in a tire
Born In The Camp With Six Toes was sleeping in the
icebox

Baby Gauge said "Be at the levee at three o'clock"

I put the robe on
I said "I almost got drowned last time"
"Going to have a mighty good time" he said
"Going to be an eclipse" Born In The Camp With Six
Toes said

I rode the hog to church

I took the new shoes off
I lit the candles
I changed the book
I rung the bell

I was drinking the wine
I heard Baby Gauge yell

I ran down the aisle
I saw the men at the trough
They were beating the hog over the head with sledge
hammers
It was like the clock in the German pilot's shack

One of his eyes was hanging out
And the trough was running over with blood

They held his head under the water
He was rooting in his own blood
He pumped it out in a mist
Like a buck shot in the lung
It was black

He broke loose

I ran down the road yelling
I stepped on soda bottle caps

I ran through sardine cans
I tripped on the cassock

The hog was crazy
He ran into the church
He ran into tombstones

I said "Somebody throw me something"
Chinamen threw me a knife

I ran after the hog
He was heading for the river
I jumped on his back

I rode the hog
I hugged his neck
I stabbed him seven times
I wanted the knife to go into me
He kept running
I ran the knife across his throat
And the blood came out like a bird

We ran into a sycamore tree

When the cloud passed over the moon
Like a turkey shutting its eye
I rowed out into the slew
Not allowing myself to sing gospel music

I woke up in a boat
It was full of blood
My feet were dragging through the water
A knife was sticking in the prow
And the sun was black

It was dark

But I saw the snake doctors riding each other
I saw my new shoes
I put them on
They filled up with blood

I took the surplice off
I threw it in the river
I watched it sink
There was hog blood in my hair

I knelt in the prow with the knife in my mouth
I looked at myself in the water
I heard someone singing on the levee
I was buried in a boat
I woke up
I set if afire with the taper
I watched myself burn
I reached in the ashes and found a red knife

I held my head under the water
        so I wouldn't go crazy
It was some commotion
I rowed the boat in a circle with one oar

A hundred people were in the water
They had white robes on
Some of them had umbrellas

They jumped up and down on the bank
They rowed down the levee

They were yelling and singing
One of them saw me
I saw a horse with tassels

I put my head under the water
I thought I was dead
I hit it on a cypress knee

Two Negroes came riding through the river
They rode towards me on the moon-blind horse

One of them was drinking soda water
"Where are you going, boy" Baby Gauge said

The horse swam back to the levee
I was with them
The boat drifted away
A man said "Shadrach, Meshach, and Abednego"

III Hambone

They tied his hind legs together
And hung him in a tree with a log chain

I saw them
I was on Baby Gauge's horse
I threw a knife at the midget
So they hung me up by the feet too

I saw them break his neck
I saw them pull his legs apart

like a wishbone
I wished the dead came back

The midget stood on a bucket
He reached up in the hog's throat
And pulled the heart out

The dog was lying on the ground
With his mouth open
It took all day to butcher the hog

I got dizzy
I saw the snake doctors riding each other

They turned the bucket over
It filled up with blood

They made a fire

The guitar player beat his hand over his leg
He put some meat on the fire

They tried to make me eat it
The midget spit a bone on the ground

The other one picked it up
He put it on his finger

He went over and got this guitar
He tried to play it like a Negro
There was too much grease on his hands
He got blood on the guitar

The midget danced around the campfire

I wanted to cut his throat

The dog bayed at the moon
And the blue Andalusian rooster played with a snake
I was bleeding out my nose

The fish bandits loaded the hog on Baby Gauge's horse
They threw blood on the fire
And filled the bucket up with guts for fish bait
When they rode off I yelled "Peckerwoods"

I dreamed I saw Holy Ghosts walking around the
campfire
He was a wild hog with blood on his tushes

Along about midnight I heard a boat
        but no rowing
Somebody short came walking out of the woods
With a light on his head
The light went out I couldn't see
He drew something out of his boot
He grabbed me by the hair
I saw a knife in the moonlight
"Sweet Jesus" I said

Born in The Camp With Six Toes cut me down

IV Chainsaw

The man cut his hand off at dawn
I heard him yell
I set up in bed

He ran past the window
"Don't let the dog get it" he said

I got out of bed
I had the long handles on
It was cold
I threw some wood on the fire
I put the dime around my ankle
I put my boots on
I put a knife in the boot

I walked out to the road
The blue Andalusian rooster followed me
It was dark

I heard the chainsaw in the woods
I heard him singing all night
He was cutting firewood
He was drunk

The dog quit barking

I drew the knife out of my boot
I looked for the midget
I saw the blood and I tracked it
I saw the sun and the moon
I saw the snake doctors riding each other

The hand was in the sawdust
It was moving
The hambone was on the finger
It was morning

The dog didn't get it
I did

There was blood on the chainsaw

I told the blue rooster
"He thought it was a guitar"

I walked around the hand seven times
I poked it with a stick
I sung to it
I picked it up like a snake
I took the hambone off the finger
I put Holy Ghost's bone in my boot
I put the hand on a stump

I danced on the hand
I peed on it

I broke a wine bottle over it
I threw it up in the air and a hawk
      hit it
The dog licked the blood out of the dust

I saw the fish bandit's guitar
The blue rooster pecked it
I beat the hand with it
I threw the guitar in the river

The snake doctors lit on it
It floated away

I went down to the bank
I got a pole
I put a hook through the hand
I washed it off

When I touched the wound with my knife
        it rolled up in a fist
Somebody came by in a boat
They held up a big fish
So I held up the hand

They jumped out of the boat
They thought I crossed them
One of them said "That wasn't no hoodoo, was it"
It was Baby gauge
I said "No, it was the guitar player's hand"
They swam to the bank
I told them how I came by it
Born In The Camp With Six toes said "It won't
Take another fish off my lines"

I asked them "You want to shake it"
Baby Gauge said "No, I want to spit on it"
We spit on the hand

They left

I wrapped it up in the newspaper like fish
I took it home

I put it under Jimmy's pillow
and he knocked my teeth out
I put it in a cigar box with a picture
        of Elvis Presley
I took it to town

I walked over to the dance hall
The guitar player was bleeding in the back of the pickup

I gave him the cigar box
He passed out

The midget pulled a knife on me
I picked up the hand
He ran off

On the way home I ran folks off the road
When the truck came by the house
The guitar player raised up in the bed
He said "Give me my hand back"

When it was dark
I tied fish line to it and hung it
        in the outhouse
I sung to it
The moon shined through the chink hole
on the hand

I took it down
I threw it in a yellow jacket nest
I stomped on it

I took it to the palm reader
I said "Sister, read this"

A lot of evenings I listened for them
I knew they would come back

When a stranger got a drink at night
I thought it was the Holy Ghost
And sometimes a cloud went by like a three-legged dog
And the thunder was someone with a shotgun
Letting him have it

Now the moon was a fifty-cent piece
It was a belly I wanted
        to cut open

When the flies got bad
I kept the hand in the smokehouse

V Swimming at Night

The midget ran his finger across his neck
The other one said "Give it back"

I waited in the outhouse
I had a sawed-off shotgun
The men rode off

In the afternoon they sold fish
They cleaned them at the pump
The scales dried up on their faces
They loaded the meat on the stolen horses

At night they rode up shooting pistols
I slept with an ice pick under my pillow

One night they rode up drunk
The midget was sitting in the guitar player's lap
He said "Come on out"

They tied a bale of hay to Baby Gauge's horse
They poured coal oil on it
They set it on fire
They laughed

The horse with the moon eye pranced around them
He galloped home

I carved wild hog out of a cypress knee
I made it the handle
I made four tushes out of the hambone
I used the blade I brought out of the fire
And sealed the pig with
It was the blade I put the burning horse to sleep with
I called the knife the Holy Ghost

To make me go crazy
I took all my clothes off
And jumped down the hole in the outhouse
I grabbed the yellow jacket nest
And held it over my heart
I pumped cold water over myself
And wallowed in the mud
I walked through the snake den barefooted
I swam the river at midnight
With the hand and a blue feather in my mouth

And the Holy Ghost around my neck

And the hooks caught in my arms   they caught in my
      legs
I cut the trot lines in two
I saw the guitar player stealing the fish

I was swimming beneath the shack
Under the sleeping midget
With the fish bandit's hand in my mouth

I climbed through the trap door
I crawled under the bed

I cut the hooks out
I believe I was snake bit
I put the hand in the slop jar
I reached up and tickled his nose with the feather

He got out of bed
He turned the lights on
He let down his pants
He reached under the bed for the slop jar
He took the lid off
He screamed
I brought the knife across his leg
I hamstrung the midget
I swam under the water
With the hand in my mouth

I came up near the guitar player's boat
He was running the lines

I swam to the other end of the trot line
I put the hand on a hook
I jerked the lines like a big fish

The guitar player worked his way down
He thought he had a good one

I let go of the line
He saw his left hand
He screamed
He fell out of the boat

I swam back through the river
I buried the knife in the levee

I was sleeping in the Negro's lap
He was spitting snuff on my wounds

Born In The Camp With Six Toes cut me with a knife
Baby gauge sucked the poison out
Oh Sweet Jesus the levees that break in my heart